W9-CUB-947

3D PRINTING

SCIENCE • TECHNOLOGY • ENGINEERING

BY STEVEN OTFINOSKI

CHILDREN'S PRESS®

An Imprint of Scholastic Inc.

CONTENT CONSULTANT
Matthew Lammi, Assistant Professor of Technology, Engineering & Design Education, NC State University, Raleigh, North Carolina

PHOTOGRAPHS ©: cover: William Andrew/Getty Images; 3: StockPhotoPro/Fotolia; 4 left: 3D Systems; 4 right: Hacettepe Teknokent; 5 left: Blend Images/Superstock, Inc.; 5 right: cdsb - Imaginechina/AP Images; 6: science photo/Fotolia; 8, 9: 3D Systems; 10: Cockrell School of Engineering at The University of Texas at Austin; 11 top: James King-Holmes/Science Source; 11 bottom: Cockrell School of Engineering at The University of Texas at Austin; 12: wsf-s/Shutterstock, Inc.; 13: Mandel Ngan/Getty Images; 14: Time & Life Pictures/Getty Images; 15 top: dpa picture alliance archive/Alamy Images; 15 bottom: Science & Society Picture Library/Getty Images; 16: 3D Systems; 17: HP Inc.; 18: Bloomberg/Getty Images; 20: Ole Spata/ dpa/picture-alliance/Newscom; 21: Bloomberg/Getty Images; 22: VCG/Getty Images; 23: Hacettepe Teknokent; 24 left: Jesse Knish/Getty Images; 24 right: Globe Newswire/AP Images; 25: 3D Systems; 26: Dan McCoy/Rainbow/Superstock, Inc.; 27: NASA; 28: Martin Zabala Xinhua News Agency/Newscom; 29 top: Martin Zabala Xinhua News Agency/Newscom; 29 bottom: Artur Debat/Getty Images; 30: Erik S. Lesser/EPA/Newscom; 31: Piero Cruciatti/Alamy Images; 32: VCG/Getty Images; 34: Bloomberg/Getty Images; 35: Feathered Angels Waterfowl Sanctuary/Rex Features/AP Images; 36: Andrea De Martin/ Dreamstime; 37: Blend Images/Superstock, Inc.; 38: Courtesy of Yoav Reches; 40: StockPhotoPro/Fotolia; 41: corepics/Fotolia; 42 top: Lucy Nicholson/Reuters; 42 bottom-43 bottom: AF archive/Alamy Images; 43 top: Gilles-Alexandre Deschaud/Formlabs; 44: The Washington Post/Getty Images; 45: Perry Backus/ AP Images; 46: Vince Talotta/Getty Images; 48: Marco Vacca/Getty Images; 49: Lucas Schifres/Getty Images; 50 top, 50 bottom-51 bottom, 51 top: Monash University, Information Technology and Engineering; 52: Tribune Content Agency LLC/Alamy Images; 53: ITAR-TASS Photo Agency/Alamy Images; 54 top: Underwood Archives/Getty Images; 54 bottom-55 bottom: Amnarj Tanongrattana/Shutterstock, Inc.; 55 top: cdsb - Imaginechina/AP Images; 56: William Andrew/Getty Images; 57: Olivier Douliery/ABACAUSA. COM/Newscom; 58: 3C Stock/Alamy Images; 59 top: Huguette Roe/Shutterstock, Inc.; 59 bottom: Paul Dronsfield/Alamy Images.

LIBRARY OF CONGRESS CATALOGING-IN-PUBLICATION DATA
Names: Otfinoski, Steven, author.
Title: 3D printing : science, technology, and engineering / by Steven Otfinoski.
Other titles: 3 D printing | Three-dimensional printing | Calling all innovators.
Description: New York, NY : Children's Press, an imprint of Scholastic Inc.,
    2016. | ?2016 | Series: Calling all innovators : a career for you |
    Includes bibliographical references and index.
Identifiers: LCCN 2015050833| ISBN 9780531218655 (library binding) |
    ISBN 9780531219881 (pbk.)
Subjects: LCSH: Three-dimensional printing — Juvenile literature. | Printing
    industry — Vocational guidance — Juvenile literature.
Classification: LCC TS171.95 .084 2016 | DDC 621.9/88 — dc23
LC record available at http://lccn.loc.gov/2015050833

1 2 3 4 5 6 7 8 9 10 R 26 25 24 23 22 21 20 19 18 17

Science, technology, engineering, the arts, and math are the fields that drive innovation. Whether they are finding ways to make our lives easier or developing the latest entertainment, the people who work in these fields are changing the world for the better. Do you have what it takes to join the ranks of today's greatest innovators? Read on to discover whether 3D printing is a career for you.

TABLE *of* CONTENTS

3D Systems' Cube was one of the first
home 3D printers.

3D printers have been used to create
new body parts for injured animals.

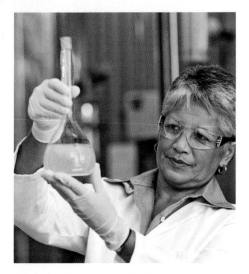

Chemical engineers look for new materials to use with 3D printers.

A 3D printer constructs a model one layer at a time.

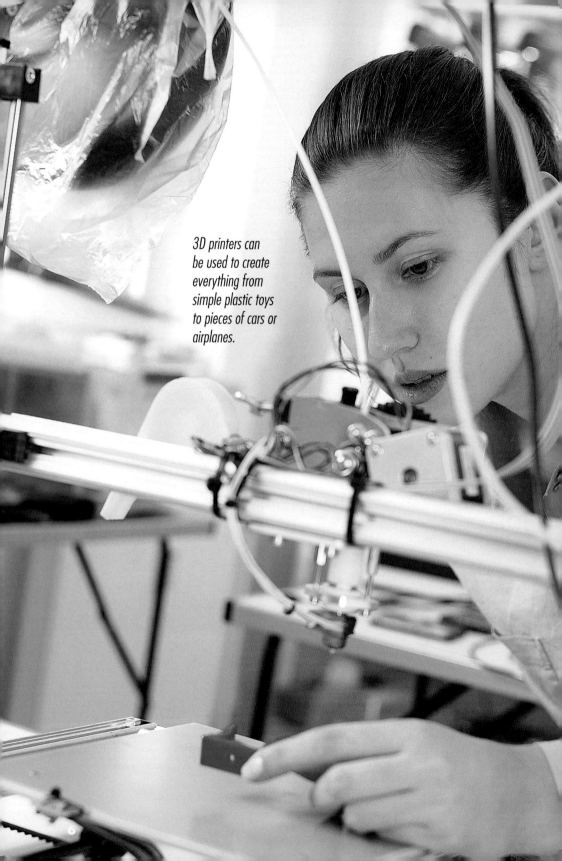

3D printers can be used to create everything from simple plastic toys to pieces of cars or airplanes.

CHAPTER ONE

A NEW KIND OF MANUFACTURING

Printing out a photo or a newspaper article is as easy as pressing a button on your family's home printer. But what if you could download and print not just a picture of an object, but the actual object itself? Sounds like science fiction? It's not. It's happening today through the amazing technology of three-dimensional (3D) printing.

The 3D printing process uses computers and special printing devices to build new products from raw materials such as plastics or metal. This fascinating technology is pointing the way toward an exciting future where anyone can design and build anything they imagine. Some experts even believe that it could completely change the way products are designed and manufactured.

THE DEVELOPMENT OF 3D PRINTING

1983	1986	1993	2005
Charles Hull creates the first 3D-printed object, a small cup.	Hull cofounds 3D Systems, the first company to commercialize 3D printing.	MIT develops its own 3D printing process, coining the term "3D printing."	Dr. Adrian Bowyer founds RepRap, an initiative to build a 3D printer that can produce most of its own parts.

HOW IT WORKS

3D printing is a complicated process. It begins with a computer program that sends digital instructions on how an object is to be "printed," or manufactured. The printer receives the instructions and squirts out a stream of heated, semiliquid material through nozzles or jets. This liquid solidifies into a thin layer. More layers are added, one by one, until they form the desired shape.

Engineer Charles Hull got the idea for 3D printing while working at a small ultraviolet (UV) parts manufacturer. The company built **prototypes** of plastic parts, but its method was expensive and time-consuming. If a prototype didn't work, it was discarded and the process had to start all over again. Hull thought this could be made easier if a quick way to develop the prototypes could be found. He began working on this new process in his off-hours.

Charles Hull shows off a car wheel created using one of his printers.

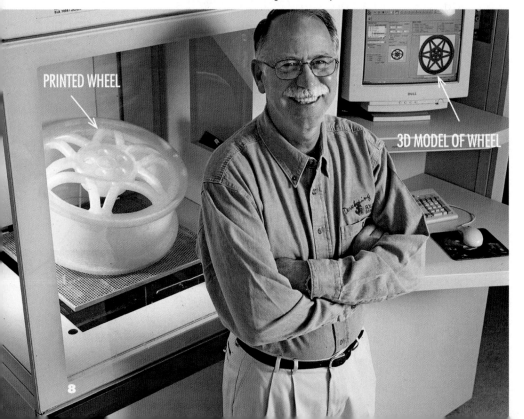

PRINTED WHEEL

3D MODEL OF WHEEL

BIRTH OF A PROCESS

The light from UV lamps can be used to solidify plastic particles into a hard covering, or **resin**, on furniture. Hull used the same process to stack thousands of layers of resin to create a complete three-dimensional object. On March 9, 1983, he created his first 3D-printed object—a small cup. Within three years, Hull had founded his own company, 3D Systems. The company set out to find customers for its prototype printing process, which Hull had called additive manufacturing.

Business was slow at first. The printers were too large to travel with. This made it hard to demonstrate them to potential clients. To solve this issue, Hull instead showed home videos of demonstrations. One of the first clients to buy the 3D printers was the automotive industry, to make prototypes of new auto parts. Other industries soon purchased the printers as well.

Charles Hull's first successful 3D-printed object was this small cup.

CHARLES HULL

The creator of 3D printing was born and raised in western Colorado. After college, Hull moved to California, where he worked as an engineer for several companies before discovering 3D printing. He served as president and chief operating officer at 3D Systems from 1986 to 1999. Still active in the company, Hull holds more than 60 U.S. **patents**. He sees himself as a member of a creative team more than a sole inventor. "I don't have a crystal ball that tells me what things are going to happen," he has said, "but I know . . . when you get enough smart people working on something, it always gets better."

PAST MARVELS

Carl Deckard (left) and Joseph Beaman (right) show off an early SLS machine in the mid-1980s.

SELECTIVE LASER SINTERING

One major difficulty in the early days of 3D printing was finding an effective way to make the individual layers of material stick together. It took an undergraduate student and a junior professor in engineering at the University of Texas at Austin to come up with the solution. In 1984, student Carl Deckard suggested to Professor Joseph Beaman that a laser could be used to melt powder between each material layer. The melted powder would fuse the layers together. Beaman was intrigued with the idea. The two went to work as a team to make the process, called Selective Laser Sintering (SLS), a reality.

SECURING FUNDS

Grant money for developing new technology was available at the university. However, Beaman realized that a project built around 3D printing—then an untried and little-known process—would not be accepted. In order to receive funding for the project, he told the university that he was working on using lasers to cut sheet metal. After two years of work and experimentation, the team gained a corporate partner, Nova Automation, that helped finance their work.

Architects use SLS to create models of the buildings they plan to construct.

AN INDUSTRY STANDARD

Beaman and Deckard perfected SLS, and it became an important part of the 3D printing process. SLS has improved over time, and it remains the standard today. In 2015, Beaman received the Inventor of the Year Award from the University of Texas–Austin's Office of Technological Commercialization. "I always tell my students engineering is really easy, because every problem we solve isn't that difficult," Beaman says. "The problem is you have to solve so many, and they all have to work." Carl Deckard cofounded a company in 2012 that develops materials for use in SLS machines. ✳ .

Professor Beaman shows off some of the objects his machines have created.

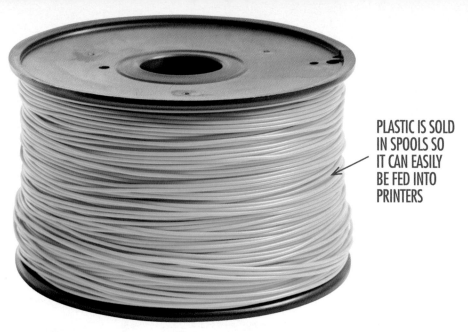

PLASTIC IS SOLD IN SPOOLS SO IT CAN EASILY BE FED INTO PRINTERS

Colorful plastic is one of the most commonly used materials for modern 3D printing.

A GROWING TECHNOLOGY

3D Systems' control of 3D printing technology lasted only a few years. In 1993, the Massachusetts Institute of Technology (MIT) developed its own 3D printer and first trademarked the term "3D printing," or 3DP. By 2011, MIT had given six companies permission to market its 3D printing process.

In its first two decades, 3D printing was used almost exclusively by large companies to create prototypes or small tools or parts. Designers created prototype objects using 3D modeling software and printed them out layer by layer. In a matter of hours, the item was complete and could be evaluated. The process saved time, money, and effort.

A new generation of printers was more compact and efficient. These printers could use a variety of materials, such as metals and ceramics, to make products. Large industries began to use the printers to create not just prototypes or parts, but actual products in large numbers at a cost far lower than traditional manufacturing.

THE GOVERNMENT STEPS IN

In 2012, President Barack Obama designated $30 million to create the National Additive Manufacturing Innovation Institute (NAMII). NAMII was organized alongside universities and businesses to improve 3D printing technology. Its main goal is to attract more manufacturing companies, especially failing ones, to 3D printing. In May 2013, the Obama administration established three additional manufacturing innovation institutes with $200 million funded from five federal agencies, including the Departments of Defense, Commerce, and Energy.

President Obama examines a 3D printer at a community workshop in Pittsburgh, Pennsylvania.

Technicians program the Electronic Numerical Integrator and Computer, also known as ENIAC, in 1946.

EARLY COMPUTERS

Before 3D printers could exist, there had to be powerful computers to run the complex software used to design objects. The first modern computers were larger than the first 3D printers. Giant computers like the Electronic Numerical Integrator and Computer, invented in the mid-1940s, could fill a large room and were powered by thousands of vacuum tubes.

INNOVATIONS

The invention of the **transistor** in 1947 made smaller computers possible because bulky vacuum tubes were no longer necessary to provide power. The first personal computers (PCs) appeared in the 1970s. However, they were not easy for beginners to use. Operating one of these computers required a great deal of specialized knowledge. The appearance of the Apple II in 1977 made home computers more user-friendly. More and more people began purchasing computers to use at home.

MACHINE OF THE YEAR

The granddaddy of laptops, the Compaq Portable computer, appeared in 1982 and weighed a whopping 28 pounds (12.7 kilograms). But PCs were finally becoming

Apple cofounder Steve Wozniak designed the hardware of the Apple I computer.

popular. In fact, they were so popular that *Time* magazine named the PC the Machine of the Year in 1983. Through the 1980s and 1990s, PCs continued to become more powerful, more compact, and easier to operate.

FASTER AND FASTER

More-powerful computers led to more powerful software. By the 2000s, artists could use their home PCs to create detailed 3D models. At the same time, the Internet became faster and more widespread. These developments would make it possible for 3D artists to create and share designs with people around the world. ✷

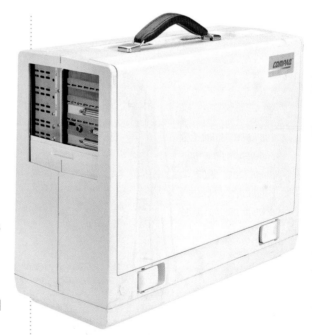
The Compaq Portable computer could be folded up and carried like a suitcase.

A WAVE OF POPULARITY

By the 2010s, the public was beginning to learn just how amazing 3D printing was. Companies were finding new ways to produce 3D printers that were cheaper and easier to use. They also began producing increasingly compact models for home use. One of the first of these home printers was 3D Systems' Cube, which went on sale in 2012. The size of a home coffeemaker, the Cube cost around $1,300. It had a port for a thumb drive and an on-off switch. Aimed for use by consumers, the Cube had its limitations. It operated like an industrial-sized 3D printer but on a much smaller scale. It could create small objects in 16 different colors of plastic. However, only one color could be used at a time. Later models could print multicolored objects. They also allowed users to print with different materials, such as various types of plastic.

The Cube's small size and appealing design made it one of the first 3D printers to become popular among home users.

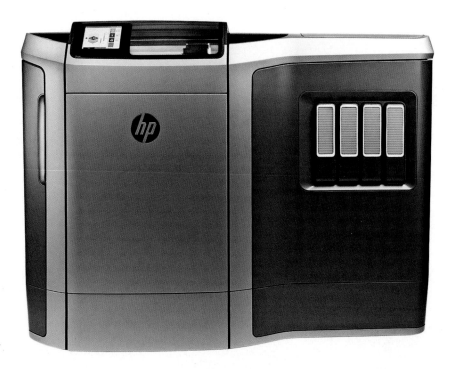

Home 3D printers like Hewlett-Packard's Multi Jet Fusion could make 3D printing available to more people than ever before.

AT THE SPEED OF THOUGHT

The "maker movement" is a group of people across the world who value designing and making, and who want to share it. Many of them create objects and devices at home using 3D printers and other technological tools. They often use discarded or broken raw materials to create their products.

The maker movement, a decrease in the cost of 3D printers, and the increased use of 3D printing by large companies has resulted in a boom for 3D printers. In 2014, almost 133,000 3D printers were shipped worldwide. That same year, Hewlett-Packard unveiled its Multi Jet Fusion 3D printer. It uses less material to create objects and is composed of lower-cost parts. This makes it more affordable to consumers and helps cut down on the amount of waste it produces.

An employee operates a large 3D printer at a company that produces prototype parts for automobile manufacturers.

CHAPTER TWO

A WORLD IN 3D

3D-printed products have come a long way from Charles Hull's first tiny cup. Today, 3D printers range in size from the portable to the giant industrial size. These machines are being used to create an incredible range of products. Major companies and small start-up businesses are cranking out precision parts, jet aircraft engines, large appliances, clothing, and even food—all made by 3D printers. Consumers are also creating their own customized products at home. They have found, in the words of *Make* magazine publisher Dale Dougherty, "Wal-Mart in the palm of your hand." When it comes to making things, the sky's the limit for 3D printing today.

3D PRODUCT FIRSTS

2010	June 2011	July 2011	2014
Urbee, the first car with 3D-printed exterior parts, is exhibited.	The first 3D-printed chocolate is produced at Great Britain's University of Exeter.	The world's first 3D-printed aircraft is flown.	Work begins in the Netherlands on the first large house to be built entirely of 3D-printed parts.

Specialized hardware can be printed to fit any user's exact needs.

CUSTOM MADE

One area of manufacturing where 3D printing has taken off in a big way is small, customized products. Perhaps you want a sculpted model of your dog. Or maybe you'd like a personalized birthday-cake topper with your own face on it. You can easily produce such objects using a 3D printing service such as Shapeways or Cubify. These services will send users a **template** so they can design their chosen objects online. Users return the completed designs. The services then print the object in the color and material chosen by the user, and mail it back at a reasonable cost.

Small 3D printers are also allowing consumers to make their own home repairs. In the past, when a cabinet handle broke or a plastic part snapped in a small appliance, the owner had to contact the manufacturer and purchase a replacement part. These replacement parts often came at a high price and might not arrive for days or even weeks. With 3D printing, a homeowner can inexpensively replace a part by using software provided by the manufacturer to scan the part, and then print it on a home 3D printer.

GOING LARGE

While small household products, machine parts, and jewelry make up an important segment of 3D print manufacturing, larger applications of 3D printing are emerging as printers become bigger and more efficient. For years printers have been cranking out parts for airplanes, military installations, and cars. But now, entire automobiles are being made with 3D printers. In 2014, Local Motors unveiled the Strati, a small open-top car that is made entirely of 3D-printed parts. The following year, Divergent Microfactories produced the Blade, which it called "the world's first 3D-printed supercar." The Blade's aluminum **chassis** weighs 90 percent less than the average car chassis. It also takes far less material and energy to produce a Blade than a traditional automobile. This makes the car's manufacturing process very environmentally friendly.

Local Motors' Strati car is displayed at an auto show in 2015.

HOUSES AND BRIDGES

3D printers can even be used to create buildings and other large structures. Chinese developers have constructed a five-story apartment building with 3D-printed materials. In Amsterdam, architects are in the midst of a three-year project to build a 13-room house from 3D-printed parts. A giant 3D printer is slowly building honeycomb blocks that will fit together to eventually form the complete house. Space for pipes and wiring is left in the middle of each block. "The building industry is one of the most polluting and inefficient industries out there," says project spokesperson Hedwig Heinsman. "With 3D printing, there is zero waste, reduced transportation costs, and everything can be melted down and recycled."

If a house, why not a bridge? In another part of Amsterdam, designers are building a pedestrian bridge over a canal using 3D-printing robots. Starting from opposite banks of the canal, two robots are printing multiple lines that will meet in the middle by 2017. "The symbolism of the bridge is a beautiful metaphor to connect the technology of the future with the old city, in a way that brings out the best of both worlds," says Dutch **entrepreneur** Joris Laarman.

Developers in Suzhou, China, created entire buildings by 3D-printing recycled materials.

JAW PIECES DESIGNED TO FIT
TURTLE'S FACE PERFECTLY

Thanks to 3D printing, this sea turtle was able to use its jaw again after a serious injury.

MEDICAL AND HEALTH CARE

3D printing has revolutionized the health care industry. Biomedical companies are using 3D modeling and printing to produce customized hearing aids, false teeth, **prosthetic** limbs, and even human skulls. One patient had 75 percent of his skull replaced by a plastic implant created by 3D printing. 3D models of internal organs help doctors design better surgical procedures. They also provide medical students with realistic models for practice and reference.

Veterinarians are using 3D-printed prosthetics such as legs, wheels, and webbed feet to replace missing limbs on pets and wild animals. A sea turtle injured in a boating accident off the coast of Turkey in 2015 had 60 percent of its jaw destroyed. The turtle was fitted with a 3D-printed artificial jaw made of metal.

Ping Fu speaks about Geomagic to a crowd in 2013.

A MAGIC PEN

With Geomagic's software, designers use a pen-like tool to outline their digital model, while actually feeling its surface textures. "It's like working in digital clay," said former director of marketing communications Rachael Dalton-Taggart. "The program lets designers create particularly complex and highly detailed organic shapes." These shapes can be used to make everything from custom-designed medical prosthetics to finely sculpted jewelry. Geomagic was so successful it was purchased in 2013 by 3D Systems, a top company in the industry.

GEOMAGIC SOFTWARE

Few companies have done more to advance 3D printing software than Geomagic. Founded in 1997 by Chinese American entrepreneur Ping Fu and her husband, Herbert Edelsbrunner, Geomagic is a pioneer in sculpting, modeling, and scanning software. Unlike previous 3D printing software, Geomagic gives digital designers feedback they can feel while creating their computerized models.

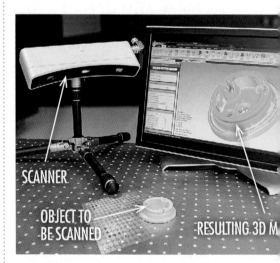

SCANNER

OBJECT TO BE SCANNED

RESULTING 3D M

Geomagic can quickly scan a physical object to create a 3D model.

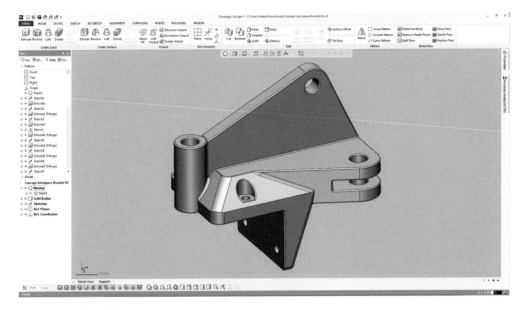

Geomagic's software allows users to easily modify scanned 3D models.

PING FU

Ping Fu, the brains behind Geomagic, was born in China in 1958. In 1984, she came to the United States, where she got a degree in computer science from the University of California at San Diego. She and her husband founded Geomagic in Illinois and later moved the company to North Carolina. It took a while for their innovative software to take off, but the wait paid off when Geomagic became a huge success. Fu published a memoir, *Bend, Not Break*, in 2013 that describes her early years in China.

AN ARCHAEOLOGIST'S TOOL

Geomagic software has also been used outside the field of product design. One of its most intriguing applications is in the field of **archaeology**. Archaeologists found clay plaques in ancient Italian sanctuaries. However, the plaques were broken into fragments. Using Geomagic software, archaeologists were able to scan the pieces and rearrange them to form complete 3D models. The 3D models were used to create physical reproductions of the ancient plaques. This gave the archaeologists a better understanding of how these artifacts were made by ancient people.

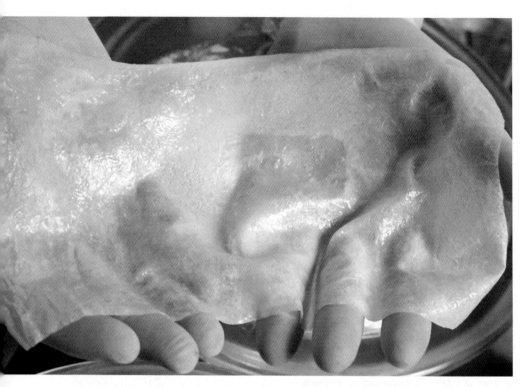

3D-printed skin could make it much easier for patients to recover from injuries.

MAKING SKIN

Researchers have not yet perfected the printing of working human organs that can be used for transplants. However, they have been able to make usable human skin. Up until now, scientists have created new skin by growing skin cells in a laboratory. However, the process is long, difficult, and prone to error. With 3D printing, they can squirt cartridges of cells from a printing head and use computer guidance to build skin faster and more precisely. The resulting skin is often a better match for the patients who need it.

3D-printed skin also has other uses. Cosmetic and drug companies can use this skin to test their products to see if they have any harmful results. This could help cut down on the number of potentially dangerous tests performed on animal and human subjects.

INTO SPACE

3D printing has recently left Earth for outer space. Two American companies have contracted with the National Aeronautics and Space Administration (NASA) to provide astronauts on the International Space Station (ISS) with tools and parts they need. The astronauts make their requests directly from the ISS. Back on Earth, a design team creates prototypes of the requested objects. These prototypes are sent to NASA officials for review to ensure they will work with the complex and sensitive equipment aboard the ISS. If a design is approved, it is then sent to the ISS. Astronauts download the designs and print out the tools on their 3D printers. These printers create objects using a high-grade plastic that counters the effects of zero gravity in space.

Astronaut Barry Wilmore shows off a 3D-printed tool created aboard the ISS.

3D-PRINTED TOOL

FROM THIS TO THAT

3D-printed toys and art are displayed at a printing café in Buenos Aires, Argentina.

3D PRINTING CAFÉS

Internet cafés, where people can bring their laptops and access the Internet while enjoying coffee and dessert, have been around since the 1990s. Recently, 3D printing cafés have added a new twist to the classic Internet café. At these cafés, you can make your own 3D-printed objects as you enjoy a drink or a snack. 3D printing cafés have popped up around the world in cities such as London, Tokyo, Berlin, and Barcelona. The United States has only a few of them, mainly because 3D printing services are widely available through small businesses. Café customers pay as little as a few dollars for a half hour of printer use. They may make a piece of jewelry or a small toy

they can take home. At DimensionAlley in Berlin, Germany, many customers make small figurines of themselves or family members and give them as holiday gifts.

A RELAXING ATMOSPHERE

Many of the café goers are beginners at 3D printing. They find the relaxing atmosphere of the café a good place to learn how to use this exciting new technology. Employees help them use their laptops or smartphones to scan images of the objects they want to make. The scanned designs are then uploaded to a 3D printer that slowly produces the physical objects layer by layer before a customer's eyes.

WORKSHOPS AND PRINTERS FOR SALE

Some cafés offer 3D printing workshops and classes for beginners and advanced students. Customers who get bitten by the 3D printing bug can even buy their own printer at DimensionAlley, which sells the devices in association with Sharebot, an Italian manufacturer. Even while enjoying their own printers at home, some customers, such as college student Alex Marschall, still like coming to the café to print. "There's a big difference in doing it on your own at home and being in an environment where you have that kind of exchange and inspiration," he says. ✴

Some cafés allow visitors to create 3D models of their own heads.

These figures were created at a café in Barcelona, Spain.

3D FASHIONS

3D printing has also invaded the world of fashion. Dutch designer Iris van Herpen has brought 3D-printed dresses to fashion runways. Israeli fashion designer Danit Peleg has created stunning women's clothing with intriguing and intricate geometric patterns. Peleg uses a flexible material called FilaFlex to make her original creations. The pieces are made section by section using 3D printers and then assembled into a complete outfit. For now, the labor and time spent on making 3D clothing is impractical for large-scale commercial production, but Peleg believes that will change as printers improve. She predicts that one day in the near future "customers could download the patterns, just like music files, and print them."

3D-printed shoes are already being commercially marketed with great success. Companies like Feetz take photos of a customer's feet and then combine this data with the person's weight, height, and physical activities. The printer takes in all this information and produces a pair of personalized shoes that fit perfectly.

3D-printed clothing by designer Iris van Herpen is displayed at a museum in Atlanta, Georgia.

Food companies use 3D printers to produce interesting designs using chocolate and other ingredients.

3D FOOD

3D-printed food is still in the early stages of development. However, it could one day be an excellent way to feed people while using less energy and resources and producing less waste. The chocolate maker Hershey signed a contract with 3D Systems to "keep moving our timeless confectionery treats into the future." The result: 3D Systems' ChefJet Pro prints an assortment of candies and other desserts.

While the focus so far is on sugary sweets, Natural Machines in Barcelona, Spain, has developed a home food printer that may be able to produce everything from pasta and pizza to chicken nuggets. "Our big vision is that we actually do see that the 3D food printer will become a common appliance in every kitchen, similar to . . . microwaves," says cofounder Lynette Kucsma.

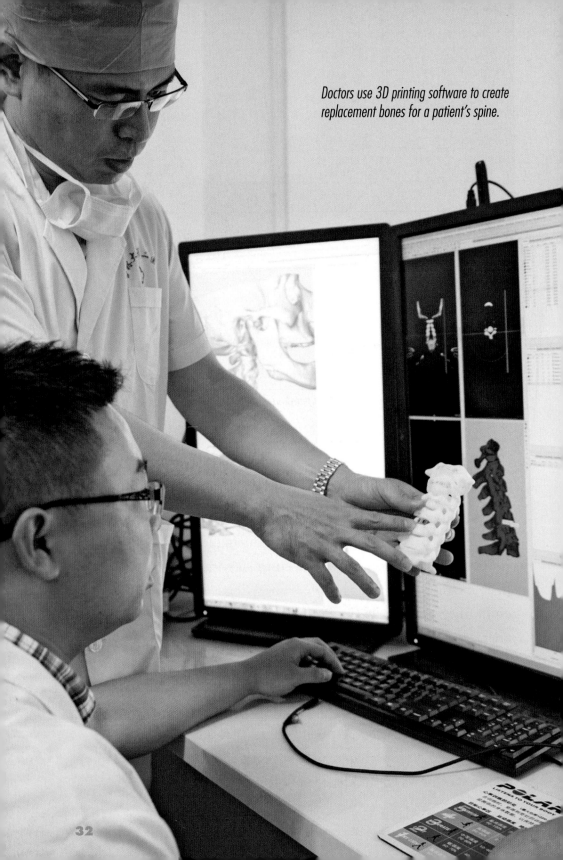

Doctors use 3D printing software to create replacement bones for a patient's spine.

CHAPTER THREE

ON THE JOB

By 2020, experts predict that 3D printing will be a $5.2 billion industry. Between 2012 and 2017, it is expected to grow 14 percent annually. That means there will be thousands of new jobs in every area of the business, from engineers and scientists to designers and entrepreneurs. The technology is so new that employers in various fields who are pursuing 3D printing can't fill positions fast enough. Whether you want to work for NASA making spacecraft, help create the latest medical devices, or even just design cool-looking decorative objects, knowledge of 3D printing could lead to a successful career. Job seekers who understand 3D printing technology will have little trouble finding work in an exciting and cutting-edge industry.

3D TECHNICAL ADVANCES

1988
The first commercial 3D printer goes on sale.

2013
The world's first 3D printing pen, 3Doodler, is invented by WobbleWorks.

2014
Hasbro teams with 3D Systems to produce toy printers for children.

Programmers must keep a close eye on their code to avoid any errors that would make a program work incorrectly.

SOFTWARE DESIGNERS AND PROGRAMMERS

Without good software to create product designs, 3D printers could not turn out their amazing array of products. Some software designers develop the applications that allow users to create 3D models on their computers. Others create the systems that operate printers or allow them to communicate with computers. Designing and printing 3D models can be a complex process. It is the job of software designers to make their programs streamlined and user-friendly without sacrificing useful features.

Software designers work closely with programmers to bring their ideas to life. Programmers write the code that makes up a program. This code is written in special languages that computers can understand. It serves as a set of instructions for a computer.

3D MODELERS

3D modelers specialize in creating digital models of objects to be printed. 3D modelers must consider every aspect of a project in their design. They must carefully review the kinds of materials that will be used to print an object. They must also ensure that the object will be the correct size, shape, density, and weight for its intended purpose. If the object will be made of multiple pieces, the pieces must fit together perfectly.

3D modelers rely heavily on their knowledge of specialized computer software. They also use their knowledge of math and physics to help design products that are sure to function correctly. They also need to understand the limitations of the printers they use. Each kind of printer has limits on the size of objects it can create, which materials it can use, and more. In many fields, 3D modelers may also need strong artistic abilities. This will help them create models that look good once they are printed.

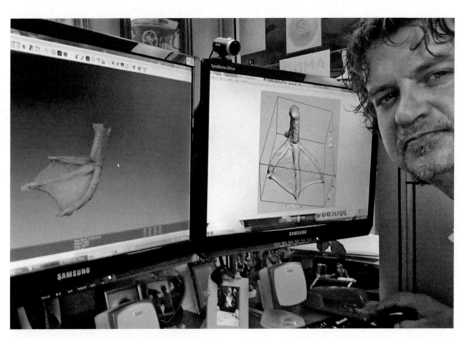

A 3D modeler creates a model of a duck foot so it can be printed and attached to a one-footed duck.

MECHANICAL AND CIVIL ENGINEERS

Many of the 3D printing jobs that will be created in the coming years will be for engineers. These positions will call for many different types of specialists. For example, mechanical engineers work on designing new 3D printing mechanisms or redesigning existing ones. They develop prototypes of printers and test them. Then they analyze the results and change the design of a printer if necessary. Finally, they supervise the manufacturing of the printers.

Civil engineers play a role in the use of 3D printing to build houses, bridges, and other large structures. They ensure that 3D-printed materials will be strong enough to support the huge amounts of weight these products involve. They also work to find new ways 3D printing might make large construction projects cheaper, easier, or more environmentally friendly.

An engineer makes adjustments to a 3D printer.

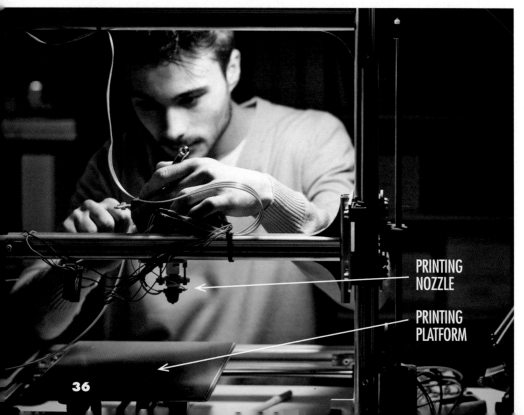

PRINTING
NOZZLE

PRINTING
PLATFORM

MATERIAL, CHEMICAL, AND BIOCHEMICAL ENGINEERS

As 3D printers continue to evolve, so are the materials that they use to create products. A wide array of materials, from plastic to concrete, is being used already, and material and chemical engineers will likely find ways to print objects using many other materials in the future. These experts will test materials that are lighter, more flexible, stronger, and more environmentally friendly to use in the printing process. They will also help solve any issues that currently prevent certain materials from working with 3D printers.

Perhaps no area of 3D printing is more exciting than biomedicine. Biochemical engineers are already experimenting with creating human tissue using 3D printing technology. One day, doctors might be able to print out body parts needed for transplants and other procedures at the press of a button.

Searching for new materials could enable 3D printers to create items that are stronger, less expensive, or more environmentally friendly.

Yoav Reches is the leading product designer for Formlabs, a 3D printer manufacturer in Somerville, Massachusetts. His job involves creating not only 3D printers, but also the parts and tools that go with them.

When did you first realize that you wanted to be a designer in 3D printing? Did any person or event inspire that career choice?
I grew up in Israel in a very creative atmosphere. My father was an architect and my mother a ceramic artist and later a graphic designer. From an early age, I was very interested in the arts. In school I tried everything—painting, sculpture, poetry. Above all, I loved making and designing things. Much later I discovered that 3D printing could allow me to design anything that I could imagine.

What kinds of classes did you take in high school and college to prepare for your career? I took art and design classes in high school and got a bachelor's degree in product design. I chose it because of the diversity of materials I could work with in designing products. I later earned a master's degree in London.

What other projects and jobs helped you prepare for your career in 3D printing?
At 16, my father introduced me to a man who ran a unique arts performance ensemble called the Zik Group. The group's artists would build huge sculptures, including puppet figures, in front of live audiences, and then would burn some of them. I spent 12 years working with Zik

Group. I started out as a gofer and ended up the company's manager. It was a great learning experience for me. I came to realize the importance of collaboration and the group dynamic that develops between artists working toward a common goal.

What projects have you worked on that you're especially proud of? I don't have a particular project, but I did experience a moment of inspiration that affected how I look at my work. One day in my studio, I found I had no tool to cut a piece of plastic. So I took a hacksaw and cut the plastic. It worked great. I suddenly realized that the tool used to make a piece could be as important as the piece itself. That's what 3D printing is all about. The printer is a tool that can make almost anything.

It takes a team of people to produce 3D printing. Does working as part of a team come naturally to you? Yes, I've come to realize that teamwork is essential to my work. So much more force and purpose and joy results when you share and learn from the experiences of others. Teamwork is about dropping your ego level and allowing the power of the team to take over.

Let's say someone gave you whatever you needed to design and build your dream 3D printer. What would it look like and what would it do? Having unlimited access to 3D printing in my work is the fulfillment of my dream. I enjoy the creativity and freedom to work with the printer every day. My goal is to design printers that meet all the needs of users.

What advice would you give to a young person who wants to work in 3D printing one day? I would tell them to go as wide as you can in your studies, not necessarily deep. Follow your curiosity and work in a variety of creative areas. By doing this, you will have the opportunity to work on many different projects. When I am looking for a young person to hire in our company, I look for someone who has enough broad knowledge to be able to work in a diversity of areas. I look for someone who is curious about everything and who never stops exploring and learning. ✳

Researchers experiment with the latest technologies in an effort to improve 3D printers.

RESEARCH AND DEVELOPMENT

Research and development (R&D) workers find the best way to utilize 3D printing for a wide range of products at a reasonable cost. They might work for either private companies or governments. They investigate industries where 3D printing can be applied to create new products. Then they report their findings to their employers. When their plans are accepted, they might help develop these new products in the marketplace.

Up until recently, companies involved with 3D printing have spent relatively little on R&D, but that is changing. In the coming years, companies will spend millions upon millions of dollars improving 3D printing technology and finding new ways to use it.

ENTREPRENEURS WELCOME

In the past, it could be very complicated to set up a small business to sell goods such as jewelry or toys. After designing a product, an entrepreneur would need to find a factory that could produce the goods at a reasonable price. He or she might also want to rent or buy a space in which to store the manufactured goods or a shop from which to sell them.

Today, there are many opportunities for forward-thinking entrepreneurs to set up small businesses based on 3D printing. All someone needs to start manufacturing products is an idea, a good printer, and knowledge of how to operate it. Many owners of small 3D printing businesses don't even have office spaces or storefronts. They simply make their products at home and sell them over the Internet.

Starting a 3D printing business does not require a lot of space or money.

THE ARTISTIC SIDE

Directors Anthony Stacchi (left) and Graham Annable (right) and producer Travis Knight (center) led in the creation of LAIKA's The Boxtrolls.

Nowhere else in the popular arts has 3D printing had a greater impact than in stop-motion animation. Stop-motion animation takes more time and effort than any other animation technique. An animator moves physical puppets and background objects a tiny bit at a time by hand. A photograph of the scene is taken each time. A single second of a stop-motion movie requires 24 of these photographs. As a result, the average stop-motion animator produces only one to two minutes of film per week. While 3D printing has not sped up this process, it has made the puppets and their movements more expressive and lifelike than ever before.

LAIKA COMES ALIVE

LAIKA, an animation company based in Portland, Oregon, was the first to use 3D printing to make its films. The animators scanned in a hand-sculpted puppet and printed out multiple versions of it, each with a different facial expression. Each printed version can also move differently. The characters come to life as never before using this process. "The advantage to this process is that you get the wonderful performance and subtlety normally reserved for CG [computer generated] animation in a stop-motion animated film," says director Brian McLean. LAIKA's success with 3D printing can be measured by the Academy

Gilles-Alexandre Deschaud's Chase Me *premiered in 2015.*

Award nominations it has received for films such as *Coraline* and *ParaNorman*. The company's latest film, *Kubo and the Two Strings*, based on a Japanese myth, was released in 2016.

A ONE-MAN MOVIE

French digital artist Gilles-Alexandre Deschaud has also used 3D printing to help produce stop-motion animation. For Deschaud's short film *Chase Me*, he built 2,500 3D-printed pieces. One object, an old, gnarled tree, took a week to print in 22 separate pieces that were then joined together. The entire film took 10 months of continuous printing and 6,000 hours of labor. "I wanted to bring 3D printing technology to the art of stop-motion animation to create a new kind of film," Deschaud has said. ✳

Coraline was nominated for Best Animated Feature Film of the Year at the 2010 Academy Awards.

TRAINING AND EDUCATION

3D printing is such a new technology that few colleges and universities offer degrees in the field. Most people interested in pursuing careers in 3D printing will need to gain experience on the job. However, they will likely need a college degree first. Engineers, software developers, and 3D modelers will need a bachelor's degree to get hired for most positions. Designers should start in the industry at any level they can, just to get hands-on experience.

Even though you might not be able to earn a college degree in 3D printing yet, there are still plenty of ways to learn about the technology. You might have access to a 3D printer at your school. Or maybe you know a friend who has one. Start making your own 3D models and printing out objects. Any experience you have with 3D printing can help you get hired when it comes time to find a job.

A professor at the University of Nevada, Reno, works on a 3D printer with an engineering student.

Elementary students in Hamilton, Montana, watch as a 3D printer creates an object.

BACK TO SCHOOL

One area where education is catching up with 3D printing is the biomedical field. Colleges in Australia, the Netherlands, and Germany offer master's degrees in 3D bioprinting. Anyone hoping to learn more about 3D printing in general can turn to the online communities of "makers." While not offering formal courses, they do have strong support groups and often share projects with each other. Some high schools, and even some elementary schools, are offering 3D printing classes.

One student project completed at an Italian school gained international attention. Called MANIpulate to Communicate, it uses a 3D-printed robotic hand to teach sign language to children with hearing disabilities.

3D printing can be used to create elaborate jewelry designs.

PLASTIC, 3D-PRINTED PROTOTYPES

FINISHED RINGS

CHAPTER FOUR

FROM START TO FINISH

Making a product using a 3D printer can be a complicated process with a number of steps. But compared to traditional manufacturing, it is very simple. This is particularly true with small decorative items, such as jewelry. An ancient craft going back thousands of years, jewelry making is traditionally done by hand. It can take many hours of labor to produce a single piece. But 3D printing has cut out some of the steps and sped up the time needed to make many kinds of jewelry. It also has permitted a level of customization that was rarely possible in the past. Let's look at how one piece of jewelry is produced using the 3D printing process, from conception and design to production and the finishing touches.

LANDMARKS IN 3D BIOPRINTING

2002	2009	2012	2015
The Wake Forest Institute for Regenerative Medicine bioprints the first human kidney prototype.	A 3D-printed prosthetic knee costing only $20 is created.	A 3D-printed prosthetic jaw is implanted in an 83-year-old woman.	Researchers create working 3D-bioprinted blood vessels.

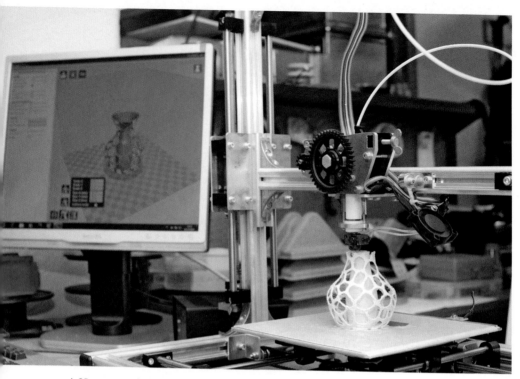

A 3D printer makes an exact replica of the design created in 3D modeling software.

A UNIQUE DESIGN

Your mother's birthday is coming up and you want to get her something special. She loves jewelry, so you decide to get her a pendant for a necklace. Your mother is fond of snowflakes, so you decide on a snowflake design. At first, you think of going to a jewelry store. However, you recently read about an online 3D printing service that makes custom jewelry. You saw snowflake jewelry in their catalog. Every piece is unique, just like real snowflakes. Even better, the company says it can personalize any piece. You decide to have your mother's name and birth date engraved in the snowflake design. You also get to choose what material the piece will be made of. You've noticed that your mom likes silver jewelry, so you choose the option for a silver pendant.

FROM DESIGN TO PROTOTYPE

To customize your jewelry design, you will use special software created by the 3D printing company. When you first open the program, it shows the basic snowflake design. You can spin the snowflake around and see it from any angle. There are tools to help you add a variety of customizations. You add the text you want engraved on the pendant. It all shows up right away on the model on-screen, so you can see what the final product will look like.

When you're finished, you submit the design to the 3D printing company and finalize your order. The company prints out your design as a plastic prototype and mails it to you. Only after you've seen the prototype and approved it will they make the final silver pendant. This step allows you to make sure that the design is just right.

An employee at a Chinese jewelry company watches as a new piece of jewelry is printed.

WHERE THE MAGIC HAPPENS

Xinhua Wu (right) shows off some items created by high-end 3D printers at Monash University in Australia.

AUSTRALIAN RESEARCH COUNCIL

Some of the most impressive research and development in 3D printing today is coming from down under. The Australian Research Council (ARC) Research Hub for Transforming Australia's Manufacturing Industry through High Value Additive Manufacturing is located in Melbourne, Australia. The center is a state-of-the-art facility located at Monash University, one of Australia's largest universities.

IMPROVING THE WORLD WITH 3D PRINTING

Under the leadership of Xinhua Wu, a professor of materials engineering at the university, the research hub has brought together top experts from several major areas to test and develop new ways of using 3D printing in science and the arts. One thing they are exploring is the use of 3D printing to create more environmentally friendly manufacturing practices. "Technological advances in additive manufacturing also bring significant environmental benefits, allowing the creation of more lightweight products which require reduced energy to produce, and a significant reduction in material waste," says professor Aidan Byrne of ARC.

The latest printers at the research hub can be used to create precise, detailed designs.

BIOMEDICAL MATERIALS

Monash University also houses the Biomedical Materials Translational Facility, where researchers are making great strides in using 3D printing to produce human tissues that can repair damaged body organs. Their innovations could lead to major changes in the way certain illnesses and injuries are treated. ✳

A researcher works with a 3D printer at Monash University.

FROM WAX MOLD TO METAL

Once you have approved the plastic prototype, workers at the 3D printing company will begin the process of creating the final silver jewelry. First, they create a mold in the shape of the prototype using a type of plastic called silicone. When the mold is finished, they pour melted wax into it. When the wax dries, it looks like the plastic prototype. The wax pendant is placed inside a container called a flask. The rest of the container is packed with sandy material to form a mold around it. The flask is placed inside a hot **kiln**, where the wax is burned away. This leaves the shape of your pendant design inside a hardened mold. The flask is removed from the kiln, and molten silver is poured into it. The metal hardens as it cools inside the mold. After several hours, the pendant is removed from the mold. Workers polish it to make it shiny and smooth. They then package it to be sent to you.

A wax cast has the same shape the final jewelry will have.

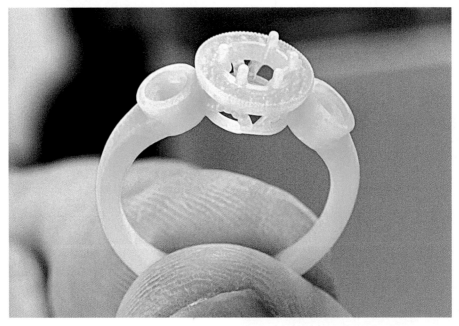

A variety of 3D rings are displayed at an exhibition in Moscow, Russia, in 2014.

SCALING DOWN THE DESIGN

When your snowflake pendant arrives, it is everything you hoped it would be. Your dad is so impressed by it that he wants to give your mom a set of earrings with the same snowflake design for their anniversary, a few months away. This is not a problem for the 3D printing company. With a few clicks of the mouse, they can scale down your pendant design for the earrings. They could also make your design into a ring or even a bracelet if you wanted.

As for your mother, she is so pleased with her pendant that she wears it every day. You start thinking about the next 3D-printed gift you'll get her when the holidays roll around.

LASTING CONTRIBUTIONS

Office workers pose with a printer in 1951.

INKJET PRINTER HEADS

3D printing is similar to traditional printing in many ways. Perhaps the biggest similarity is the inkjet printer head—the device used to spread the liquid materials that eventually harden into an object. The idea of a printing device used to squirt ink goes back to 1867 in England, when an early version of an inkjet was used to record **telegraph** signals. The first commercial inkjet used in a computer printer appeared in 1951. It could recreate an image by propelling droplets of ink onto a sheet of paper.

INKJETS IN 3D PRINTING

The same idea behind the inkjet remains key in several 3D printing processes. In material jetting, liquid material is applied in droplets through a small nozzle to build a layered object. In binder jetting, invented at MIT in 1993, there are two materials dispensed from the nozzle: a liquid and a powder. The powder helps bind the liquid molecules together to form a solid layer of material.

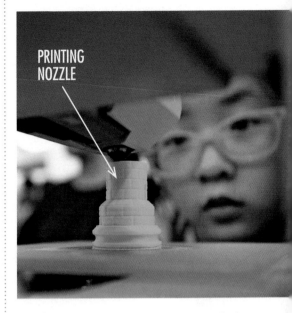

PRINTING NOZZLE

Like inkjets, the nozzles of 3D printers move back and forth to place material where it is needed.

A NEW KIND OF NOZZLE

Unlike the inkjet nozzles of traditional printers, nozzles in 3D printing range in size and shape depending on the specific product being made. For example, companies specializing in 3D food printers have had to create special nozzles for different kinds of food. ✳

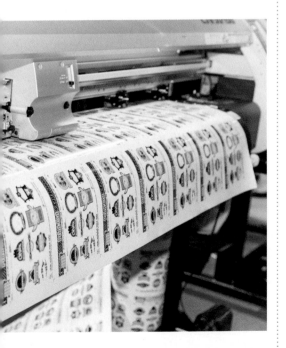

Modern ink printers can quickly reproduce detailed, colorful images.

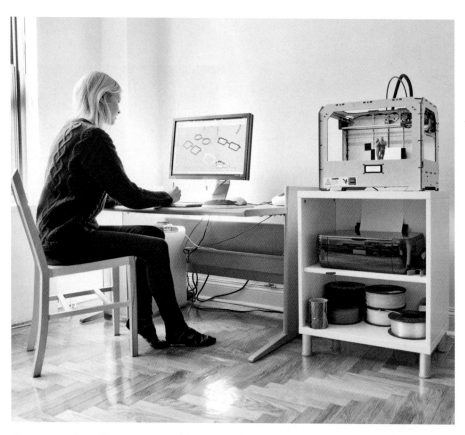

Many people share 3D printing tips and designs in online communities.

DOING IT YOURSELF

If you didn't want to go to a 3D printing service for your jewelry piece, you could create your own by buying a home 3D printer. Online do-it-yourself, or DIY, groups share their knowledge of object-making with people all around the world. If you need tips on how to create something or ideas for new projects, you won't have any trouble finding people on the Internet who are willing to help out.

You can also visit the Web site Thingiverse, which is one of the largest collections of 3D printing projects, patterns, and 3D models. You may find that the design you need has already been created. All you need to do is download it and print it out.

CLASSES AND PUBLIC ACCESS

If you want professional help designing jewelry or other small objects, you can sign up for an online class. These classes offer everything from videos and live question-and-answer sessions to homework assignments and feedback from expert instructors.

If you don't want to spend the money to buy your own 3D printer, check out your local community college, university, or vocational school. Many now have 3D printers available to anyone who wants to use them. One day, these printers might be as commonplace in libraries as copy machines.

The sky is the limit when it comes to 3D printing. What will you create?

More and more libraries are offering 3D printers for visitors to use.

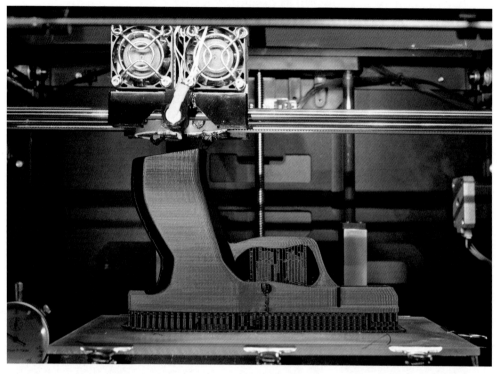

Lawmakers are trying to find ways to prevent people from using 3D printers to create dangerous weapons.

JUST THE BEGINNING

While 3D printing technology has made incredible strides in the last few years, some experts say this is just the tip of the iceberg. They predict that in the coming decades, life on Earth will be radically changed by this amazing technology.

A CHANGED WORLD

Thanks to 3D printing, many countries will no longer need to import essential resources from outside their borders. With 3D printing, it will be possible to make almost any product domestically with few wasted materials. Some industries, such as construction and agriculture, could be totally transformed as 3D printing simplifies the making of buildings and provides new sources of food. Human life itself could also be affected. Scientists foresee the day when additive manufacturing will be able to make bioprintable organs to replace worn-out and diseased ones. This could extend the average human life span by many years.

The materials used in 3D printing could add to the world's growing waste problems.

POTENTIAL PROBLEMS

As 3D printing becomes more common, there will be new challenges to face. When anything can be printed, where will we draw the line? Some people have already created plastic 3D-printed guns that can escape detection when passing through security checkpoints. Federal laws have made these weapons illegal, but what other illegal devices may be created by people using 3D printing irresponsibly?

When printers allow anyone to become a "maker," what will happen to the skilled craftspeople who devote their lives to making things? Will they find themselves out of work? And while 3D printing will eliminate much of the waste of building and construction, what will we do with the nonrecyclable plastic that is commonly used in 3D printing projects? Will it create an environmental disaster in the future as discarded prototypes and products pile up in landfills? Many people feel that the potential benefits of 3D printing will make up for these problems and that new solutions will be found. In any event, there may well be no stopping this next industrial revolution. ☀

Many factory jobs could disappear due to 3D printing technology.

CAREER STATS

SOFTWARE DEVELOPERS

MEDIAN ANNUAL SALARY (2015): $100,690

NUMBER OF JOBS (2014): 1,114,000

PROJECTED JOB GROWTH (2014–2024): 17%, much faster than average

PROJECTED INCREASE IN JOBS (2014–2024): 186,600

REQUIRED EDUCATION: Bachelor's degree

LICENSE/CERTIFICATION: None

COMPUTER PROGRAMMERS

MEDIAN ANNUAL SALARY (2015): $79,530

NUMBER OF JOBS (2014): 328,600

PROJECTED JOB GROWTH (2014–2024): -8%, decline

PROJECTED INCREASE IN JOBS (2014–2024): -26,500

REQUIRED EDUCATION: Bachelor's degree

LICENSE/CERTIFICATION: None

MECHANICAL ENGINEERS

MEDIAN ANNUAL SALARY (2015): $83,590

NUMBER OF JOBS (2014): 277,500

PROJECTED JOB GROWTH (2014–2024): 5%, as fast as average

PROJECTED INCREASE IN JOBS (2014–2024): 14,600

REQUIRED EDUCATION: Bachelor's degree

LICENSE/CERTIFICATION: Yes

Figures reported by the United States Bureau of Labor Statistics

RESOURCES

BOOKS

Bernier, Samuel N., Tatiana Reinhard, and Bertier Luyt. *Design for 3D Printing*. San Francisco: Maker Media, 2015.

Murphy, Maggie. *High-Tech DIY Projects with 3D Printing*. New York: PowerKids Press, 2015.

O'Neill, Terence, and Josh Williams. *3D Printing*. Ann Arbor, MI: Cherry Lake Publishing, 2013.

FACTS FOR NOW

Visit this Scholastic Web site for more information on 3D printing:
www.factsfornow.scholastic.com
Enter the keywords **3D Printing**

GLOSSARY

archaeology (ahr-kee-AH-luh-jee) the study of the past, which often involves digging up old buildings, objects, and bones and examining them carefully

chassis (CHAS-ee) the frame of a vehicle, on which the body is assembled

entrepreneur (ahn-truh-pruh-NUR) someone who starts businesses and finds new ways to make money

grant (GRANT) an amount of money given by an organization or government for a particular purpose

kiln (KILN) a very hot oven used to bake or dry bricks, pottery, or other objects

patents (PAT-uhnts) legal documents giving the inventor of an item the sole rights to manufacture or sell it

prosthetic (prahs-THET-ik) an artificial device that replaces a missing part of the body

prototypes (PROH-toh-types) the first versions of an invention that test an idea to see if it will work

resin (REH-zin) an organic substance used in making plastics

telegraph (TEL-i-graf) a device or system for sending messages over long distances using a code of electrical signals sent by wire or radio

template (TEM-plit) a design or pattern that is used to create similar designs

transistor (tran-ZIS-tur) a small electronic device that controls the flow of electrical currents in items such as radios, television sets, and computers

INDEX

Page numbers in *italics* indicate illustrations.

INDEX *(CONTINUED)*

ABOUT THE AUTHOR

STEVEN OTFINOSKI has written more than 180 books for young readers, including books on forensics, computers, and rockets. He fills his recycling bins every week and uses cloth bags at the supermarket. He lives in Connecticut.